I'M SO INCREDIBLY GRATEFUL

to have you in my life!

I wrote this book about you!

All rights reserved. No part of this publication or its characters may be reproduced, distributed, or transmitted in any form or by any means, including photocopying, recording, or other electronic or mechanical methods, without the prior written permission of the publisher, except in the case of brief quotations embodied in reviews and certain other noncommercial uses permitted by copyright law.

©2025 Copyright Lisa Monias

All Rights Reserved

Printed in the United States of America

If I were going to write a book about you, it would be titled...

and it would say wonderful things like...

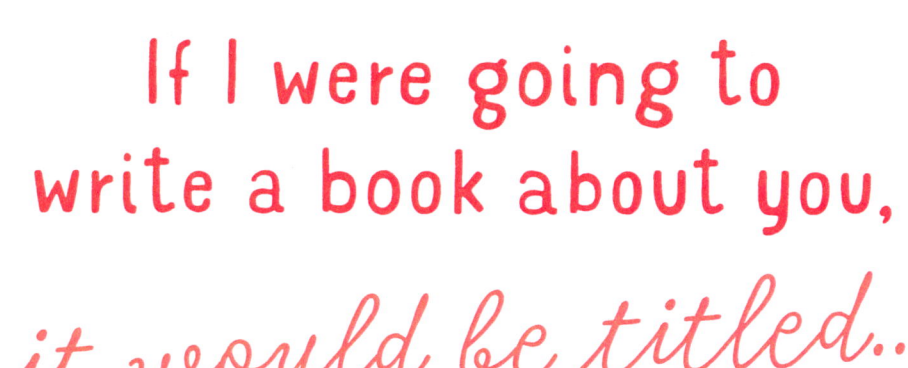

You're gold, and I *struck it rich!*

I remember the first day we met...

_____

_____

_____

_____

_____

Love • Pink roses • Puppy kisses
Hot chocolate • Warm breeze • Sunshine
Cozy hugs • Homemade cookies • Happy tears
• Laughter • Firefly nights
Twinkle lights • Birthday balloons
Snuggly socks • Bear hugs
Campfire stories • Ocean waves
Magic moments • Beautiful kindness
Giggly moments • Heart-shaped pancakes
Sparkly shoes • Fuzzy blankets
Gentle lullabies • Secret handshakes
Warm apple pie • Shooting stars • Big smiles

Three things that come to mind *when I think of you!*

1. _____

2. _____

3. _____

I could think of millions, but this is my top three!

If you were a flower

you'd be...

- ☐ A SUNFLOWER — always turning toward the light
- ☐ A DAISY — simple, cheerful, and full of joy
- ☐ A ROSE — full of beauty, love, and strength
- ☐ A WILDFLOWER — growing wherever you're needed

You'd be your own flower magic,
because you always bloomed with...

_____

You buzzed around helping everyone, just like a busy little bee!

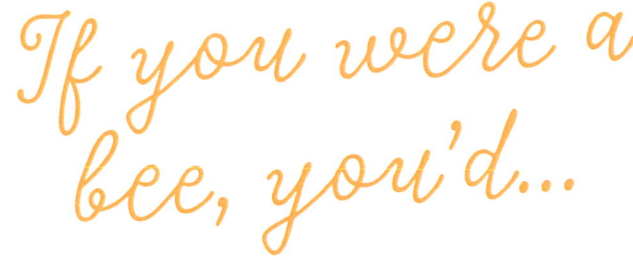

If you were a bee, you'd...

- ☐ Make honey-flavored hugs
- ☐ Pollinate kindness
- ☐ Start a hive full of love

One time you were especially "busy" helping...

_____

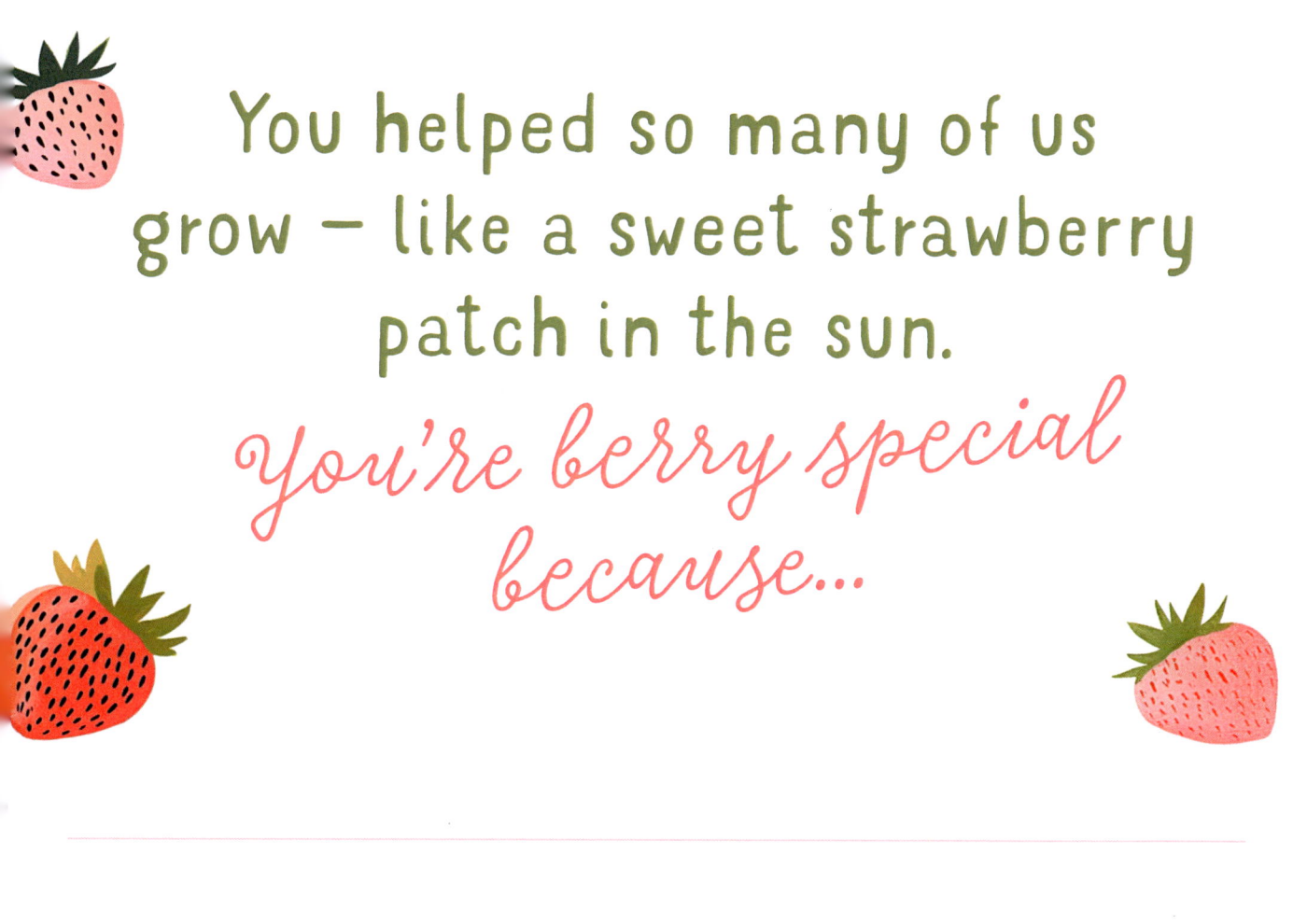

You helped so many of us grow — like a sweet strawberry patch in the sun.

You're berry special because...

_____
_____
_____
_____

Sometimes you had to
ROAR
to keep us all in line!

But you never lost your kindness.

I remember when you roared like a tiger because...

_____

You made impossible things feel possible — like a *frog that learned to fly.*

I couldn't believe it when you…

_____

_____

_____

_____

_____

You've always been LOYAL, PROTECTIVE, and KIND — like a GENTLE wolf leading the pack.

like the time you...

_____

_____

_____

_____

If we took a trip together, *we'd go to...*

- ☐ The beach, where we'd dip our toes in the sand
- ☐ The library, where we'd read all day
- ☐ The garden, where we'd smell fresh roses
- ☐ The moon, to explore new places
- ☐ Or our Dream Destination

_____

_____

Because the best adventures, are always the ones with YOU.

If I were to write a song about you, it would be called...

it would be a hit!

And the chorus would go like this...

_____

_____

_____

_____

_____

If I could invent an award for you,

it would be...

_____

_____

_____

_____

_____

If you had bat powers, *they'd be...*

- ☐ Super-sensing for when someone needed a hug
- ☐ Flying across town to deliver snacks
- ☐ Night-vision for finding lost and stray pets

I remember one "bat-time" moment when...

_____

_____

_____

You are truly incredible

I will always remember when...

Last but not least
because of you...

You are unforgettable. You sprinkle joy like confetti, dream up the sweetest ideas, and pour love into everything you do. I'm thankful to be part of your life. Keep laughing, and keep being the amazing light you are.

You probably never realized just how many lives you've touched, how many hearts you've lifted, and how many smiles you've created just by being you.

I'll bet you never stopped to think about how amazing you truly are. But now... you'll have moments of proof.

You're loved more than you'll ever know. And we're all so incredibly lucky to be part of your beautiful story.

From me, made for you!